I remember Gurlitt

A Collection of 12 Original Piano Pieces

BOOK 1

• BOOK 2

Selected and edited by
Frances Clark and Louise Goss

ISBN 0-913277-15-0

The New School for Music Study Press
Box 407, Princeton, New Jersey 08542

Preface

The piano miniatures of Cornelius Gurlitt have held a small but constant place in the affections of piano teachers throughout the 20th century. Like many prolific composers, Gurlitt often repeated himself and at times was even dull. So finding the *best* of Gurlitt was like an exciting treasure hunt. Careful culling through hundreds of his pieces revealed that at its best this is outstanding teaching material—happy, healthy music, with an occasional burst of bravura or a line of lyric loveliness.

More important, this is music that works for students. They like it at once, they can learn it easily, and they can play it beautifully. Teaching it is a joy. It has intrinsic musical worth and provides an ideal training ground for most of the musical and pianistic devices of the 19th century.

Gurlitt's life (1820–1901) spanned the Romantic Period. Born in the German city of Altona, near Hamburg, he was trained as a pianist and organist. As a young man he spent five formative years in Copenhagen, studying composition with a prominent Danish teacher, Christoph Ernst Weyse. As a result, Danish titles, styles and melodies often appear in his music.

Gurlitt served as a cathedral organist in Altona and later held an important teaching position at the Hamburg Conservatory. In Hamburg he enjoyed friendships with many of the eminent composers of the day, Schumann and Brahms among them. Schumann was said to be fond of teaching Gurlitt's piano pieces for four and eight hands, and Gurlitt's music is often reminiscent of Schumann's style.

We think you will agree that the pieces in this collection are Gurlitt at his very best, and that they deserve to become a standard part of early intermediate teaching repertoire.

Frances Clark and Louise Goss

Contents

Gavotte

Song of the Sea

March

Waltz

Allegretto cantabile

Happy Youth

Risoluto

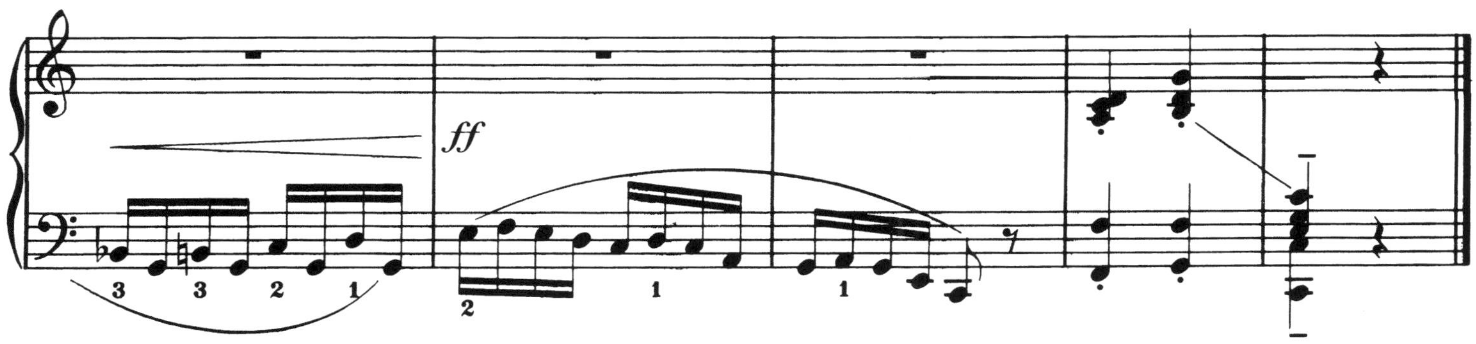

Longing

Moderato con anima

Danish Dance

Allegro

Daydreams

Grazioso con moto

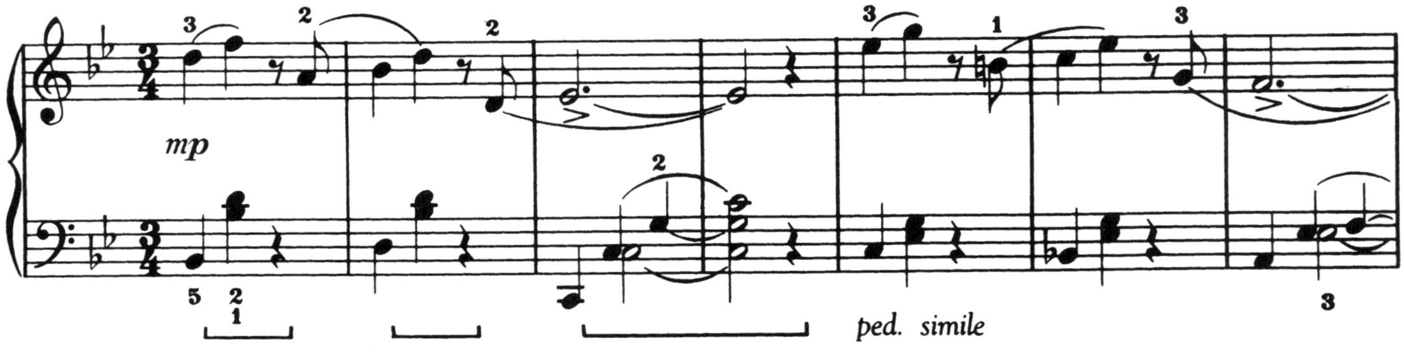

a tempo
poco rit.
mp

Little Study

Grandfather's Birthday

Brave Resolve

Allegro animato

ff
2 2 1 3 1 2
2 1
f
3 1 3 2 1 3 2 2 5 3 1 2
5
ff

Polka